Bibliographic information published by the German National Library:

The German National Library lists this publication in the National Bibliography; detailed bibliographic data are available on the Internet at http://dnb.dnb.de .

Imprint:

Copyright © 2009 GRIN Verlag, Open Publishing GmbH
Print and binding: Books on Demand GmbH, Norderstedt Germany
ISBN: 9783668355194

This book at GRIN:

http://www.grin.com/en/e-book/345370/text-linguistics-report-on-grammar-and-language-teaching

Ahmad Altasan

Text Linguistics. Report on Grammar and Language Teaching

GRIN Publishing

GRIN - Your knowledge has value

Since its foundation in 1998, GRIN has specialized in publishing academic texts by students, college teachers and other academics as e-book and printed book. The website www.grin.com is an ideal platform for presenting term papers, final papers, scientific essays, dissertations and specialist books.

Visit us on the internet:

http://www.grin.com/

http://www.facebook.com/grincom

http://www.twitter.com/grin_com

Content

Report on Grammar and Language Teaching

Introduction

The first part of this paper analyses a text by describing the following features: its social purpose and context; its audience; its register; its grammatical features at the level of the whole text i.e. its cohesion and coherence; its sentence or clause level grammatical features. Then it designs a series of grammar-focussed learning tasks which fit together in a cohesive learning program based on the text and the grammatical analysis of it, and which enhance the learners' understanding of the meaning of the whole text. The second part of this paper briefly reviews current issues in the teaching of grammar in the field of TESOL.

Chapter One: Text Linguistics

The text that is going to be analyzed in this paper is the "THE CARNIVAL" (see appendix) which is retrieved from the following website: http://www.armeniaemb.org/Kids/ArmenianFairyTales/Index.htm. See appendix 1.

1. Genre

The text is a narrative type. It is a fairy tale. It gives information about a wife and her husband in unexpected development of events. Its social purpose is to entertain and give advices and proverbs that audience may use and follow in real life. To support learning, it can be used in a school curriculum as a literary narrative type which aims to entertain through telling a story. The text has the following structure:

1. Orientation, which describes a setting in time ("Once upon a time there lived"), introduces the main characters ("a husband and his wife").
2. Complication, which gives a sequence of problematic events. It begins with that "the man bought a hundred pounds of butter and rice", and then describes the wife reaction that she gave them to the young man.
3. Resolution which deals with the attempts to solve the problem "She showed him and the man mounted his horse and rode after the Carnival."
4. Coda, which gives an overall evaluation of the events. "...came back - to find both the horse and the stranger gone. He returned home and husband and wife started fighting anew..."

The audience could be teenagers or adults who are interested in reading fairy stories. Moreover, they could be ESL learners who want to learn English through entertainment.

2. Register

The text is an interactive story. The discourse of the story is multiparty in nature as it is entirely created by three participants, (a husband, a wife and a young man). The register is informal, as it is mainly a conversation between a husband and his wife, so the vocabulary and grammar are not complex and are more characteristic of spoken language and there are a lot of informal words such as "I've"; "aren't"; "I'll"; etc. The main tone of the conversation is an argument (They were always fighting about something or other.). The argument is about a hundred pounds of butter and rice. The events happened a long time ago ("Once upon a time there lived ....") and most of the conversation took place in a house ("As she was sitting by the door ....", "The man hurried into the house ...").

3. Coherence

While doing discourse analysis two major fields have to be considered, the coherence and the cohesion of the text. Coherence is the overall construction and organization of a text "which can be viewed as part of top-down planning and organization" (Celce-Murcia & Olshtain 2000, p.8). The topic of this text is the Carnival. The author has made the text coherent by relating all the conversations to the topic. Though there are cases when a paragraph is not directly connected to the previous one, they serve the reason of creating a scene. There is coherence within paragraphs as well. The sentences are interconnected and they create a real picture of the situation. The coherence of the text is also kept by presenting new information, the comment or the theme, in a logical sequence. For example, in the first half of the text the scene is set where the reader may guess what the situation is: a man took the butter and rice and ran away. In the next paragraph, the husband mounted his horse and rode after him.

4. Cohesion

The next field of consideration while doing discourse analysis is the cohesion of the text, which Halliday and Hasan (1976) view as "the basis for coherence." To support their definition of these two concepts they further state "... cohesion is the foundation

3

on which the edifice of coherence is built. Like all foundations, it is necessary but not sufficient by itself." (Celce-Murcia & Olshtain 2000, p.125). The cohesive ties that are used in the language to connect different linguistic items in the text create cohesion. Therefore, cohesion is the bottom-up connections in a text (Celce-Murcia & Olshtain 2000). There are grammatical and lexical ties. Grammatical ties in their turn have four categories: *reference, ellipsis, substitution and conjunction*. Through the bottom-up approach to text analysis many cohesive ties, both lexical and grammatical are evident which bring the texts to be cohesive.

4.1. Reference:

As Halliday and Hasan (1976) state one of the important aspects of cohesion is the ability of hearers and readers to identify the relevant portion of text as referent when they are faced with references (personal, demonstrative). One of the factors that enable them to do this is the internal cohesion within the passage that is being presupposed. In this text, endophoric (anaphoric) references are mainly used, where the reference follows the referent. The grammatical ties of the text are expressed through all types of references. There are different types of references in the text that make the cohesion of the text very clear. For example:

a. Personal references

> "The <u>man</u> called **his** <u>wife</u> a dimwit and **she** returned the compliment.
> **They** were always fighting about something or other."

For example, in the above sentence the pronoun 'his' is an anaphoric reference for the word 'man', the pronoun 'she' is an anaphoric reference for the word 'wife' and the pronoun 'they' is an anaphoric reference for both "man" and "wife".

b. Demonstrative references

All the distinctions have some relevance to cohesion, in that they particularly determine the use of these items in endophoric (textual) reference.

Demonstrative reference is also a reference by means of the location. The speaker identifies the referent by locating it on a scale of proximity. The existential demonstrative *here* refers to the location of the house.

> "Hey, brother, come **here** for a minute!"

"The man saw at once that ***there*** must be something wrong...."

The meaning of 'there' is anaphoric and locative. Another example: 'That' is endophoric, cataphoric reference to following text.

"Well all I have to say is ***that*** after all we're not your servants..."

"Why so angry, my dear? ***That***'s just I've come for."

4.2. Ellipsis

Ellipsis is the omission of a grammatically required linguistic item the existence of which is made clear by the context of the text. Celce-Murcia & Olshtain (2000) differentiate three types of ellipsis: nominal, omission of a noun; verbal, omission of a verb; and clausal, omission of a clause. The cases of ellipsis observed in the text are the following:

"You are not *the Carnival* by any chance, are you {the carnival}, brother?"

"Why {are you} so angry, my dear?"

"Our man, however, walked on and on and finding nobody {the man} turned round and came back"

The word 'the man' is an ellipsis. The author has omitted it but it is clear from the

first part of the sentence that the doer of the action is the same person that is *the man*.

4.3. Substitution

Substitution is the use of the word 'one' to substitute for another word. This is to avoid the repetition of the same word in the same sentence.

"Good day, brother. Have you seen a ***man*** going this way?" "Yes, indeed, I did see ***one***"

The word 'one' used to substitute the word 'a man'

4.4. Conjunctions

Conjunctions are the words that are used to connect different parts of sentences or different sentences. As there is a lot of conversation in this piece of discourse, there are many occurrences of the use of conjunctions. For example:

"What did you go ***and*** buy so much butter ***and*** rice for?"

"Some time passed ***and*** the woman waited ***and*** waited, ***but*** the Carnival did not come."

"I've been looking for your house for a long time *but* couldn't find it."

4.5. Lexical cohesion

Synonyms: e.g., furious = angry; galloped = mounted; returned = came back; escaped = took off his village; catch up = grab

Antonyms: e.g., cry # laugh; rode # climbed off. Repetition: e.g., butter and rice

4.6. Text connectives

According to Droga & Humphrey (2003), text connectives hold the text together by making the sequence of the events explicit for the reader.

"Our man, **however**, walked on and on and..."

"Maybe **then** you'll catch him up".

"**Meanwhile**, the Carnival, making good his escape,"

5. Morphology

Morphology is the study of the internal structure of words. The morpheme is the smallest meaningful unit in English (Huddleston & Pullum, 2005). Examining the text, there are different types of morphemes: a free base morpheme 'man', free non-base morpheme 'The' an inflectional bound morpheme ' fight<u>ing</u>', a derivational bound morpheme 'kind<u>ness</u>', a compounds' <u>forehead</u>' and clitics ' It<u>'s</u>'.

6. Word classes

Identifying a word in terms of its class help us to know how these individual words combine to make meaning (Droga & Humphrey, 2003). The text contains many types of words: a noun 'man', a pronoun 'she' a verb ' live', an adjective 'dimwit', an article 'the', a preposition ' by' and a conjunction 'and'.

7. The tenses

As to the time used in this text, it can be divided into two parts **the narration** and the **direct speech**. The basic time axis of the narration is the past simple with rare uses of the past continuous to state the situation.

> Once upon a time there *lived* a husband and wife who *did* not see eye to eye. The man *called* his wife a dimwit and she *returned* the compliment. They *were* always *fighting* about something or other.

> As she *was sitting* by the door one day, she *saw* a man hurrying by along the street. She *raised* one hand to her forehead and *called*:

In the direct speech, however, the present simple is the basic time axis with occasional uses of the present perfect, the present continuous, the present prefect continuous, the simple past and the future to connect what they had at the moment of speech with coming events.

> "What *are* you *talking* about? what funeral banquet, what wedding?" (Present continuous)

> "Aha, I'*ll say* I am, and see what happens". (Simple future)

> "Why so angry, my dear? That's just I'*ve come* for. I'*ve been looking* for your house for a long time but couldn't find it."

> "What *did* you go and buy so much butter and rice for?"

The selection of this time creates link between the past, the moment of speech and the future. It helps the readers have a clear picture of the event discussed providing them information which would not be clear otherwise.

8. Auxiliary verbs

There are two types: modal auxiliaries and non-modal. Examples from the text:

Modal = "*are* you talking"; "I'*ve* come"; etc.

Non-modal = "there **must** be"; "I **can** catch him up"; etc.

9. Phrases and Words

A simple sentence consists of (one or more) constituents called phrases, and each phrase consists of one or more constituents called words. There are many types of phrases: a verb phrase, a noun phrase, an adjective phrase, an adverb phrase, a preposition phrase, etc. Examples from the text:

"The man called his wife a dimwit"	
Name	Words
Noun phrase	"The man"
Verb phrase	"called"
Noun phrase	"his wife"
Adjective phrase	"a dimwit"

10. Sentences and Clauses

There are two types of clauses: an independent clause which has subject and predicate and can stand alone as a sentence and dependent clauses which express a complete thought but cannot stand alone, so that it is not a sentence.

Independent clauses:

The most common type is **the canonical clause**, which consists of a **subject** and a **predicate**. Examples from the text:

name	structure	Example from the text
Ordinary intransitive	S-P	"The young man stopped."
Complex-intransitive	S-P-PC	"The wife calmed down"
Ordinary monotransitive	S-P-O	"she returned the compliment"
Complex-transitive	S-P-O-PC	"The man called his wife a dimwit"
Ditransitive	S-P-O-O	"I gave him back his things"

Dependent clauses (Subordinate clauses)

Finite subordinate clauses:

Name	Example from the text
Noun clause (reported speech)	"Well all I have to say is **that after all we're not your servants...**"
Adjectival clause (Relative clause)	"there lived a husband and wife **who did not see eye to eye**"
Adverbial clause (conditionals)	"Well, **if you like**, you can leave your horse with me..." "Do you think I can catch him up **if I ride fast**?"

Non-finite subordinate clauses:

Name	Example from the text
To-infinitival	"Why haven't you ever showed up **to take your stuff away?**" , "Well all I have **to say**"

Bare infinitival	"Do you think **I can catch him up** if I ride fast?"
Gerund-participial	"I saw him **coming along the road**", "Aren't you ashamed of yourself, **taking advantage of our kindness?**"
Past- participial	"Why haven't you ever **showed up** to take your stuff away?"

Adjuncts

Adjuncts are unlike complements, they do not have to be licensed by the verb. There are different types of adjuncts which function as an adverb phrase, a preposition phrase (PP), a noun phrase (NP), a finite clause and a non-finite clause.

Name	Function	Example from the text
Frequency	Adverb	"They were **always** fighting about something or other."
Time	PP	"When the husband came home **in the evening**"
	NP	
Condition	Finite clause	"Do you think I can catch him up **if I ride fast?**"
Purpose	non-finite clause	"Why haven't you ever showed up **to take your stuff away?**"

11. Types of sentences

A. Simple sentences:

A simple sentence consists of only one independent clause. Examples from the text:

"His wife was furious"

B. Compound sentences:

A compound sentence consists of two or more independent clauses. For example:

"The man called his wife a dimwit **and** she returned the compliment."

D. complex sentences:

In a complex sentence the main clause combines with one or more dependent clauses (subordinate clauses). For example:

"she saw a man hurrying by along the street."

"there lived a husband and wife who did not see eye to eye"

12. Speech acts types

Name	Example from the text
Declarative	"It's for the Carnival".
Open interrogative	"What are you talking about?"
Closed interrogative	"Did he go by long ago?"
Imperative	"Take it and put it all away."
Exclamatory	"Didn't I always say you were a dimwit!"

13. Learning tasks

Learners

The students are intermediate-level learners. They know the basic vocabulary of the text, they are familiar with skimming and scanning reading skills, and they are able to participate in discussions on different topics. They are learning English for academic purpose.

The aim

The purpose is to develop students' interactive reading skills and their knowledge of grammatical features that make the text meaningful.

Number of students: 15

The grammatical features I am going to incorporate into this learning program are:

Cohesion: The text has many lexical and grammatical ties such as references, conjunctions, and synonyms. Moreover, it uses text connectives to hold the text together

Tenses: the text can be divided into two parts the narration and the direct speech. In the narration part, it uses the past simple with rare uses of the past continuous to state the situation. In the direct speech, however, the present simple is the basic time axis with occasional uses of the present perfect, the present continuous, the present prefect continuous, the simple past and the future to connect what they had at the moment of speech with coming events.

Dependent clauses: The text uses noun clauses, relative clause and adverbial clauses to express important details such as time, place, manner, etc. The text uses many adverbial clauses, thus I will focus on them only.

My intention is to make my students familiar with some of the features of discourse and raise their consciousness of the use of the linguistic elements. With the help of this text, I try to draw their attention to linguistic items that they do not notice or they notice unconsciously. Through this text, I intend to enable them to practice their reading skills and be acquainted with the use of the language in real communication.

Task (1) Jigsaw activity (rearrange the paragraphs)

I will divide the text into 15 strips. Each student is given a strip from the text; they read their part and retell it to the class. When retelling I will write some key words or phrases on the board and numerate them according to the paragraph the students are retelling. The students do not have the paragraphs in sequence. They listen to each other carefully. Meanwhile I will put down the key words and expressions on the board. After finishing the retelling of the whole text, the students try to form the whole story with the help of the key words and phrases written on the board and the information they received from their peers. They arrange the paragraphs in order. After rearranging the paragraphs, the students are given the text and they compare the order of the text with the original one. Then class feedback takes place. Students point out the clues that helped them to find the links between the paragraphs. Some explanation takes place based on what makes the text to become meaningful.

Task (2)

I will distribute the handouts and ask students to find the passages in the text where the names of the heroes are mentioned for the first time and write the sentences containing them. Tell them to read their examples and have a discussion on how they realized who is who. This is to make students realize the different cases of the use of pronouns and synonymous words. Then ask students to find conjunctions in the text and discuss their importance by taking out the sentence from the context and writing on the board. Discuss the additive function of 'and' and contrasting function of 'but'. In this way, students see more clearly the importance of conjunctions as cohesive ties. Examples:

(References)

"The _man_ called **his** _wife_ a dimwit and **she** returned the compliment. **They** were always fighting about something or other."

(Conjunctions)

11

"What did you go *and* buy so much butter *and* rice for?"

"I've been looking for your house for a long time *but* couldn't find it."

The aim of the two tasks above is to explain students that they cannot express the meanings they want if they do not tie their ideas correctly, they will confuse their reader or the listener.

Task (3) I will use another fairy story (only one paragraph), which has the same grammatical features of the carnival (direct speech and reported speech), to practice the tenses.

Choose the correct forms of the verbs in the following text.

Once upon a time there {**lives** / **lived**} a king. This king {**announced** / **will announce**} through his country: "The one who {**told** / **tells**} such a lie that I say "It's a lie" {**will get** / **got**} the half of my realm ".A shepherd came and {**says** / **said**} : "Long live the king! My father {**had** / **has**} such a bludgeon that he could reach to the sky and mix the stars with it".

Test (4): Complete the conditional sentences using any suitable idea:

1. If the president visited me, _____.

2. I won't enjoy the party if _____.

3. I'd be very happy if _____.

4. If he continues to tell lies, _____.

5. He wouldn't have got lost if _____.

6. If I could travel in time, _____.

7. If the water reaches 100°C, _____.

8. If he hadn't drunk so much alcohol, _____.

Chapter Two: Current issues in grammar teaching

According to Ellis (2006), Grammar teaching "involves any instructional technique that draws learners' attention to some specific grammatical form in such a way that it helps them either to understand it metalinguistically and/or process it in comprehension and/or production so that they can internalize it (84)". The most challenging problem which many English language teachers face is how, to what extent, and even whether to teach grammar (Celce-Murcia, 1991). Although researches on second language acquisition (SLA) have helped much, there are a number of controversial issues that need to be solved.

Prescriptive and Descriptive

One major issue in grammar teaching was the instructional balance between prescriptive and descriptive grammars in classroom implementations (Celce-Murcia, 1991). Linguists call the grammar books, which we are used to, prescriptive: that is, they prescribe rules for proper usage. For several hundred years, "grammar" was synonymous with "prescriptive grammar." Traditionally syllabuses have been based on structural or descriptive grammars, but Linguists today have not found such models useful and have preferred to rely on modern descriptive grammars (Ellis, 2006). Descriptions of how people really speak and write, instead of rules on how they should.

Moreover, the choice of which grammatical features to teach is controversial. According to Krashen (as cited in Ellis, 2006) "grammar teaching should be limited to a few simple and portable rules such as 3rd person–*s* and past tense–*ed* that can be used to monitor output from the acquired system." In contrast, many researchers reported that learners are capable of mastering a wide range of explicit grammar rules (Ellis, 2006). To solve this issue, Ellis (2006) argued that we should distinguish between two senses, the difficulty of understanding a grammatical feature and the difficulty of using it accurately in communication. These two senses relate to the distinction between learning grammar as explicit knowledge and as implicit knowledge

Explicit or Implicit

The debate over the place of grammar in instruction has played a major role in the history of language teaching. In Krashen's Monitor Theory (as cited in Ellis, 2006) he distinguished "acquisition" and "learning". He argued that although second language (L2) learners might be exposed to explicit rules in classrooms, grammar instruction played no role in acquisition. In contrast, Norris and Ortega's (as cited in Ellis, 2006) metaanalysis of 49 studies, revealed that grammar instruction was effective for both acquisition and learning.

Deductive or Inductive

In discussing this issue, a distinction is often made between deductive (Harmer, 2007: "explain and practice" pp. 203) and inductive (Harmer, 2007: "discover and practice" pp. 207) grammar teaching. Deductive grammar teaching is a "grammar is given" approach i.e. T presents a grammar rule/structure and then Ss practice. Inductive grammar teaching is a "grammar is discovered" approach. T provides Ss with samples of the target form and allows them to work out the rule for themselves (Harmer, 2007). Examining the relative effectiveness of these two approaches to teaching explicit knowledge, some researchers found that a deductive approach was more effective, while others reported a clear advantage for inductive approach (Ellis, 2006).

Intensive or Extensive

Intensive means teaching grammar over a sustained period of time focusing on a single grammatical feature or a pair of contrasted structures (e.g., English past continuous vs. past simple). On the other hand, Extensive grammar teaching means focusing on a whole range of structures within a short period of time (e.g., a lesson) so that each structure receives only minimal attention in any one lesson (Ellis, 2006). The present-practice-produce (PPP) model of grammar teaching, which is used in most grammar books, is an example of the intensive approach. In extensive approach, teachers provide corrective feedback in the context of both form-focused and meaning-focused lessons (Ellis, 2006).

Communicative approaches

Language teaching has gone through many changes in terms of methodologies used. First, the traditional approaches, which focus on the mastery of grammar and then the communicative language teaching CLT, emerged. The main principle of all communicative approaches is that the learner must not only know how to make a grammatically correct structure, but must also improve the ability to use language to carry out various real-world tasks (Nunan, 1988).

According to Richards (2005), there are different current approaches which can be viewed as falling within the general framework of communicative language teaching: Process-based CLT approaches (content-based instruction & task-based instruction). Product-based CLT approaches (text-based instruction &competency-based instruction).

Text-based approach (TBI) is mainly concerned with what learners do with whole texts in context. It is concerned with units of discourse called texts (Feez, 1998). In addition, Celce-Murcia (1991) suggested that grammar teachers teach grammar in a discourse context. According to this view, learners in different contexts have to master the use of the text types occurring most frequently in specific contexts. These contexts might include: studying in an English medium university, studying in an English medium primary or secondary school, working in a restaurant, working in an office, etc. (Richards, 2005).

Components of texts, such as grammar, vocabulary, topics and functions usually are specified in a mixed syllabus, which integrates reading, writing and oral communication and which teaches grammar through the mastery of texts rather than in isolation. For example, the Certificates in Spoken and Written English, which are widely taught language qualifications in Australia, include the following text-types: exchanges, forms, procedures, information texts, story text and persuasive texts. (Richards, 2005).

Task-based approach (TBI) makes tasks as the central unit in the learning process. The rationale behind this approach is that by focusing on the completion of the task, students will learn language in the same way if they are focusing on language forms (Harmer, 1988). Its advocates claim that second language acquisition (SLA) research can and should guide second language instruction. The purpose of such research is to enable designers to determine the types of tasks that can best facilitate acquisition of specific target language structures and functions (Loschky & Bley-Vroman, 1990).

Tasks such as listing tasks, sorting and ordering, comparing, problem solving, etc. are the basis for TBI. Traditional classroom activities such as drills, cloze activities, etc.

15

are not recommended in TBL. The advocates of TBI also claim that students do not achieve progress in their grammatical development through a PPP methodology (presentation, practice and production) because language learning result from meaningful interaction using the language and not from controlled practice (Richards, 2005).

References

Celce-Murcia, M and Olshtain, E. (2000). *Discourse and Context in Language Teaching: A Guide for Language Teachers.* Cambridge UK; New York: Cambridge University Press.

Celce-Murcia, M. (1991). Grammar pedagogy in second and foreign language teaching. *TESOL Quarterly, 25*(3), 459-480.

Droga, L. & Humphrey, S. (2003). *Grammar and meaning: an introduction for primary teachers.* Berry, N.S.W: Target Text.

Ellis, R. (2006). Current Issues in the Teaching of Grammar: An SLA Perspective. *TESOL Quarterly, 40*, (1), 83-107.

Feez, S. (1998). *Text -based Syllabus Design.* Sydney: National Centre for English Teaching and Research.

Halliday, M. A. K. and Hasan, R. (1976). *Cohesion in English.* London: Longman.

Harmer, J. (2007). *The practice of English language teaching.* (4th ed.). UK: Pearson Longman.

Huddleston,R. & Pullam, G. (2005) *A student's Introduction to English Grammar.* Cambridge, NY: Cambridge University Press.

Loschky, L. & Bley-Vroman, R. (1990). Creating structure-based communication tasks for second language development. *University of Hawai'i Working Papers in ESL,* 9 (1), 161-212.

Nunan, D. (1988). *The Learner-Centered Curriculum: A Study in Second language Teaching.* New York: Cambridge University Press.

Richards, J. C. (2005). Communicative language teaching today. Singapore: *RELC,* 1-44.

Appendix 1

THE CARNIVAL[1]